Fifty Nifty Money Making Ideas

50 Ideas for Starting a Profitable Home Based Business to Make Extra Cash

By

Karen J Cornwell

To accomplish great things, we must not only act, but also dream; not only plan, but also believe

Contents

I have decided not to include a contents page in this book.

This is to encourage you to read the whole book to find the perfect idea to start you on your way to earning the extra cash that you want.

From the ideas listed, there is *at least* one that could be making you money right now

After reading the book remember that you have to actually TAKE ACTION rather than simply *thinking* about it.

This time next year you could be running a very lucrative home based business if you take the time to plan carefully and go for it!

To make it to the top, you must take the

first step.

Fifty Nifty Money Making Ideas

50 Ideas for a Profitable Home Based Business

Do you hate your job?

Do you have to get up every morning to drag yourself to the office?

Are you looking for ideas to supplement or even replace your full time income?

Or Are You…

- Currently 'between jobs' and finding it difficult to land a job in today's uncertain economy?

- Retired and want to supplement your income?

- A stay at home Mom and could do with a little extra cash?

- A student who needs cash to help finance your education – or even your social life?

Whatever your reason for wanting to make a little bit of extra cash, this book will have something that you can implement RIGHT NOW to get you started and something to plan for future cash generation.

Still with me?

Right, let's get on with it, there is cash out there just waiting for you to make a start…

I will begin with some very simple ideas, but do read the whole book where you will find some very interesting (and easily do-able) ideas for making some extra money.

ONE

Sell all Your Unwanted Household Stuff.

Just have a quick look around your home and see how much stuff you really have. Do you use or enjoy everything?

A general rule that I use to determine if something is still useful to me is – have I used/worn it in the past 12 months?

If the answer is 'No' then it goes into a box or pile to be sold.

Remember, *one mans junk is another mans treasure*, so even things that you think will not be of use to anyone could bring in a bit of cash.

Have a look in the garage, the attic and that spare room where you dump everything 'until you need it'.

Even odd tools and that old box of screws could bring in a few bucks, so don't throw anything away – you could cash it in.

Ornaments that you have had for years that you no longer display could be worth something. Have a quick look on ebay to see if there is anything similar just in case it is worth more that you thought. Ebay will give you a vague idea of the value of most things if you are unsure.

What about the pictures that you have stored in the attic because you can't stand to look at them any more? They may not be Picasso or Monet but, in some cases, the frames are worth more to buyers that the picture itself.

Where to Sell Your Stuff

Have a garage sale – get the kids involved, they will love it! Advertise around the neighborhood so that people know about your sale. Put up some posters or a small advert in the local stores.

Advertise – online for free on craigslist, usfreeads or in your local free ads paper. You will be amazed at the response you will get from a small lineage advertisement.

If you have some larger items or want to sell everything in one place, you could contact an auction house to see if they will sell your items. If they think that you have something that their clients would buy, they will take it and sell it at their next auction day.

You can be sure that you will get the best possible price because most auction houses take a percentage of the selling price, so it is in their best interest to get a good price for your items. Speak to a couple of auction houses to see which offers the best deal.

Set up an eBay sellers account and list your items on there. It does involve a little internet knowledge but is really simple to do once you get the hang of it.

To sell on eBay, you should have a Paypal account - again easy to set up. The successful bidder will pay you immediately; then you simply mail the item. Don't forget to specify the cost of postage when listing your item.

TWO

Sell Garden Plants

If you are a keen gardener you could sell your surplus plants.

When you plant seeds you will always get lots more seedlings than you can use. So, instead of tipping the extra seedlings onto the compost heap, pot them up into small cheap pots to sell.

What about when you have shrubs or herbs in the garden that need to be thinned out? Divide up the plants carefully and pot up the extra to sell on.

Herbs are easy to grow and are a great seller. A lot of children would love to help with this type of enterprise and it will teach them a little about responsibility if they are encouraged to grow their own plants to sell for a bit of pocket money.

You don't need to have a huge garden to grow plants to sell. A few trays of seeds will produce masses of seedlings for you to pot on.

Where to Sell Your Plants

If there is a nursery close by, call in and see if they want to buy your plants. They usually have to buy quite large amounts of the same type of plants, so may be delighted to be able to buy a small amount at a reasonable price.

If you live on a busy street, set up a stall at the bottom of your drive. Get the children to help, most kids love to play 'shop'. You could even encourage your children to grow some plants of their own to sell.

Ask in your local store, a lot of stores sell plants and culinary herbs.

If you have a lot of healthy herb plants, ask around the local restaurants. A lot of chefs would be happy to buy your fresh herbs at a reasonable price.

Make up some hanging baskets to sell. They are always popular as it means the buyer can just take it home and hang it up.

THREE

Make Things to Sell

If you enjoy crafts, why don't you make things to sell?

Maybe you love making pots so make a few originals to sell. Speak to the proprietor of a local craft store and ask if they will display some of your work.

Hand made jewelry is always a good seller – again display in local stores.

Do you make soft toys, wooden children's toys, children's furniture, soft furnishings etc. These are all potential money makers.

When you have a good stock of your craft, you could book a table at a craft fair and sell your goods. If your first craft fair is a sell out, you can book more now that you know that there is a market for your goods.

Search online to find a list of craft fairs in your area or ask someone who sells at craft fairs themselves.

FOUR

Organize Your Own Craft Fair

Find a venue that you can hire for the day, check out availability and cost. It could be a room in a community center, a room in an hotel or maybe your church has a room that you can hire. Make sure that it has enough room to have at least 20 stalls or tables to make the event attractive to sellers and buyers.

Charge per table and specify the **maximum size** of table as some people will arrive with a *huge* table and simply expect to pay for one.

Advertise your event anywhere you can think of; free ad papers, craigslist, usfreeads, church notice board, store notice boards etc.

Do lots of advertising because your clients will book with you again if you provide them with lots of potential customers.

Design a booking form and send it to anyone who expresses an interest. Make sure that you get at least 50% payment on booking so you know they are not just 'tire kickers'.

On the day, you can have your own stall selling your crafts. You will save money by not having to pay for your own stall and at the same time, make a few dollars on everyone who books a space.

If you do not make anything yourself, you could sell drinks and snacks to your stallholders and buyers.

The weeks coming up to the holidays will almost guarantee lots of potential customers as people are looking for unusual and beautiful gifts to buy.

So be sure to book your holiday venues well in advance.

Ask your stall holders for full payment at the time of booking when selling space at these holiday time craft fairs.

You are almost guaranteed to sell all your space at the holiday craft fairs.

FIVE

Construct Craft Kits

If you know where to get good craft supplies you could put together some craft kits.

You can make a kit for any sort of craft from teddy bears to dolls houses and embroidery kits to wooden furniture.

If you make jewelry for instance, you could get together all the beads, wires, clasps etc. required to make a beautiful necklace or whatever. Put it all together in a box or bag and label it.

There are loads of people that would love to have everything ready prepared so they can just put the item together and still be able to say that they had made it themselves. These are very popular items to sell at craft fairs.

SIX

Start an Ironing Service

If you love to iron, you will not be short of clients if you offer this service.

Many busy families would love to have someone to iron their clothes. You could charge per item plus a pick up and drop off charge or you could calculate the amount of clothing that you could iron in an hour and charge a reasonable hourly rate.

Pick up the clothes and ask the client to supply you with enough hangers for their items. Or you could buy a box full of cheap hangers and charge the client for them if they don't supply you with any – you don't want to spend your time folding the newly ironed clothes.

Make up some leaflets and posters and distribute them around your area. Place a small advert in your local free ad newspaper. Chat to parents/friends when you go to pick up the children from school or chat to friends after church and casually drop in a reference to your new service. Word of mouth and recommendations are great free ways to get business.

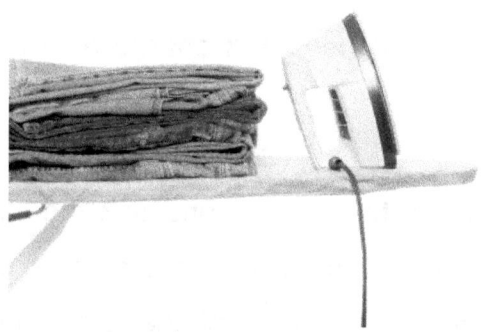

SEVEN

Hire Out Your Garage as a Rehearsal Venue.

If you live in an area where there are no close neighbors, why not clear out your garage and hire it out as a rehearsal room for aspiring musicians?

There are lots of "wannabe" rock bands that would love to have somewhere to rehearse. You could charge by the hour and only book the times when you know the inevitable noise won't disturb you and your family.

Advertise in the music stores and in the local stores that young people frequent.

Once one or two young musicians have used your garage for their rehearsal, they will pass the word round to other bands and musicians.

EIGHT

Writing Services

If you can write a simple 300 – 400 word article you can make some extra cash by writing content for websites and blogs.

You don't have to be an expert in the subjects that you are asked to write about, just do a little searching online for other articles on the required subject. For example, if you are asked to write about cooking for kids, type into Google, 'cooking for kid's articles' and you will be presented with tons of articles to give you your own ideas.

There are websites where you can advertise your services for free or very cheap, such as www.elance.com, www.digitalpoint.com and lots more. If English is your first language and you can write a good, informative article, you will have as much work as you can handle. There are however, writers from Singapore, India etc, who only have English as a second language (and it shows…) that advertise their writing services for very little money – sometimes as low as $1 per article.

Do not try and compete with these writers on price. Set a realistic starting price per article – maybe $1.50 per 100 words and stick to your guns on the price. You will need some testimonials to start, so maybe offer your first three customers a free article in return for a testimonial – if of course, they like your work!

Once you have built up a good reputation, you can begin to increase your price to a more realistic one. Webmasters are always on the look out for good writers, so you will never be short of work.

If you are good at the 'purple prose' you could offer a service on Valentines Day writing love poems for lovers to send to their 'other half' or you could even write love letters for those who would love to be romantic but lack any writing skills.

Another great benefit of this type of money making opportunity is that you can work anywhere in the world that you can get an internet connection!

NINE

Making Videos

If you have a camcorder and know how to use it, why not offer your services recording things like business presentations, school events, dog shows, horse shows etc. There are already a ton of people who specialize in weddings and christenings but would not dream of attending the local dog show.

This can be very lucrative as a lot of the dog owners would love to have a record of their dog doing a good obedience trial or a very fast agility round.

Give out your business card (you can get them for just the cost of postage from www.VistaPrint.com) to potential customers at the show and get their contact details so that you can let them know when you have transferred the class that they are interested in onto a DVD.

Record the school's nativity play and ask if you can put a note on the schools notice board, most schools will let you do this – especially if you offer to share the profit with the school fund.

You could offer your services to house sellers who may want to have a DVD that they could give to prospective purchasers or a video that they could put on a website.

Make up a couple of demonstration DVD's so that you can show potential clients your work.

It doesn't have to be technically perfect but it does need to be a good DVD that people would be pleased to show their friends.

Place an advert in the local free ads newspaper to promote your service, speak to the local schools, dog and horse owners, print up some leaflets and drop them into local business offices.

TEN

Babysitting Service

Yes, I know this is an old one – but the old favorites are sometimes the best.

What about having a service where you look after your neighbors kids whilst they go shopping, charge an hourly rate and specify a pick up time that is convenient to you both.

Evening babysitting is great for students and older people. Students will have a quiet time to do some study – as long as the children are in bed of course.

If you don't know your prospective clients, expect a lot of questions; no-one wants to leave their kids with a 'bunny boiler'.

It is a good idea to ask any other people that you baby sit for if you can give a prospective client their telephone number so they can ring for a reference.

Again, advertise in stores and your local free ad paper.

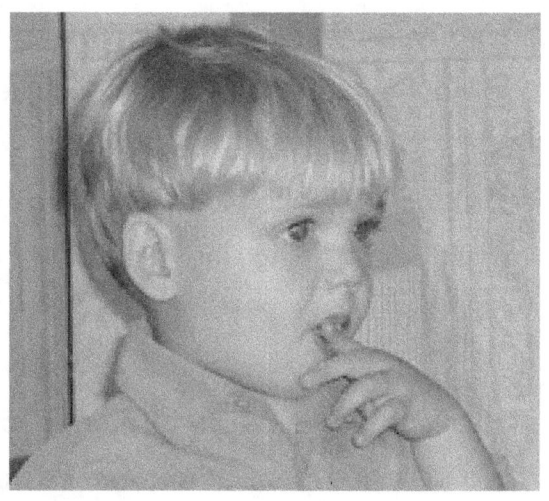

ELEVEN

Handmade Greetings Cards

There are lots of different areas to target when making greetings cards.

Lots of people love to receive a personalized card, you could make them to order or prepare a few of the more popular names to keep in stock.

You could make adult greetings cards, if you don't mind doing the research to make them unique.

Make up some packs of themed cards; animals are always a popular choice and you could even add a cute photograph of a clients own pet.

You could sell packs of your hand made greetings cards at a craft fair or visit the local stationary shops to ask if they would want to sell some beautiful and original greetings cards.

Your local store may be delighted to stock some of your unique handmade cards.

TWELVE

Calendars

There are lots of ideas for making interesting and unique calendars.

If you are proficient at using a computer, you can do everything from home or you could find a print shop that will deal with the printing side of things whilst you concentrate on the design, promotion and orders.

There are lots of topics that you could use for your design. You could offer a personalized service and make calendars featuring client's pets, children, home etc. – the options are endless.

You could sell advertising to the local businesses. Using a large template, you simply put your calendar in the center and sell the spaces around the edge as advertising.

Do a bit of research to find an acceptable price to charge for the advertising that will make the offer attractive to clients whilst still making you a nice profit. Then you give each business some free copies to distribute to their clients.

So, they are advertising all the businesses on the calendar as well as their own to their own clients. You should only include one of each type of business to make the offer attractive.

THIRTEEN

Art

Are you even just a little bit artistic?

Paint some simple abstract pictures and frame them – you even may find that you will become a sought after artist as more people buy and display your work.

It doesn't have to be an 'old master' copy; different people have different tastes in art and many love the idea of having an original work in their home.

Sell them on eBay using some really good photographs of your work.

You could speak to the proprietor of a local bar, restaurant or coffee shop and ask if they would agree to display your work.

You would attach a small, discreet price label and if any of the works are sold, the owner of the premises would get a percentage.

FOURTEEN

Compile Puzzles

Do you enjoy doing puzzles?

Could you compile a crossword puzzle? A lot of publications will pay for good crossword puzzles based on their magazine's topic.

Check out the publication first to see if they include puzzles before you spend your time compiling your puzzle. If there are no crosswords, write to them and ask if they would consider including one in their next edition. You could offer the first one free then charge for any subsequent ones.

You could write or email the publications to see if they would consider paying for your services.

Send them a sample of a puzzle that you have compiled – maybe for a competitor.

If they see that a competitor is using your work, it may encourage them to give it a try.

Some publications will want you to do a monthly puzzle for them.

FIFTEEN

Gardening Services

Another one of the 'old favorites' – but there are lots of different services to offer around a gardening theme.

A big burly student could offer to do the heavy gardening jobs whilst the older person could offer to do some plant sitting.

You don't necessarily need to offer the whole gardening package such as lawn maintenance, weeding, planting, hedge trimming etc.

You could offer to look after someone's plants in their house or greenhouse whilst they are away on holiday.

A lot of keen gardeners worry about their greenhouse plants whilst they are away from home, so this service could allow them to have a stress free, relaxing holiday.

Something else that you could offer is a "winter garden preparation" service which could include painting or re-varnishing garden furniture and fencing, repairing fencing, clearing up the fall of leaves or any other of the maintenance jobs that most people hate doing.

SIXTEEN

Making Gift Baskets

Gift baskets are a great way to earn some extra cash and could lead to a full time income if you are good at marketing your baskets.

There are lots of resources online that will show you how to make beautiful gift baskets.
You could make:

- New Baby Gift Baskets

- Corporate Gift Baskets

- Chocolate Gift Baskets

- Valentines Gift Baskets

- Children's Gift Baskets

- Birthday Gift Baskets

- Christmas Gift Baskets

- 'Just Because' Gift Baskets   (Just because – I Love You; We're Friends; You're Leaving; You're Moving and so on…)

For a New Baby Gift Basket you could put in items like talcum powder, tiny baby clothes, a soft toy or two, a beautiful shawl etc.

For a Corporate Gift Basket you could put in pencils, pens, notepads, a travel mug, a mouse mat etc.

Obviously, you would have to price these according to content, but a gift basket is a great and different gift.

You can buy a good book called "Make Gift Baskets for Profit – How to build a Profitable Business from Home" $6.99 to give you more ideas.

Go to www.createspace.com/3421386

SEVENTEEN

Home Help Service

You could offer your services as a shopper for older or infirm people. Going to the library to change books or making lunch and washing up for someone could just make a great service.

You could read to someone with failing eyesight or just spending an hour or two doing a little basic housework. You could take someone to the store to do their own shopping or offer to do all the little jobs that older people find difficult.

Set a reasonable hourly rate and ask at your local nursing home, sheltered housing complex or retirement village to see if any of the residents would like to make use of your services.

EIGHTEEN

Book Keeping Service.

If you are good at organizing, you could offer a book keeping service to local small businesses. You don't necessarily need any office skills to do this.

A lot of builders, painters and decorators, plumbers etc. will have receipts and invoices stuffed into an old bag and then panic when it comes time to do their tax returns.

You could offer to keep their books in order and charge a small monthly fee per client. Charge an initial set up fee which will cover the time taken to organize the bag of receipts, then a small monthly fee to keep everything in order throughout the year.

Each month collect the invoices and receipts and record and file them which will only take a little time once you are set up.

Doing this service for a few clients could make you a nice monthly income.

If you do have some basic office skills you could even offer to send out invoices and collect cash etc.

NINETEEN

Genealogy Research

If you enjoy doing online research, you could offer a service researching family trees. This is an area that is growing in popularity as more people are searching for their roots.

Set up a simple website offering your services, advertise in the local free ad newspapers, on craigslist, usfreeads etc.

You could offer a beautifully designed family tree drawing that people could frame and use as a gift for their family members.

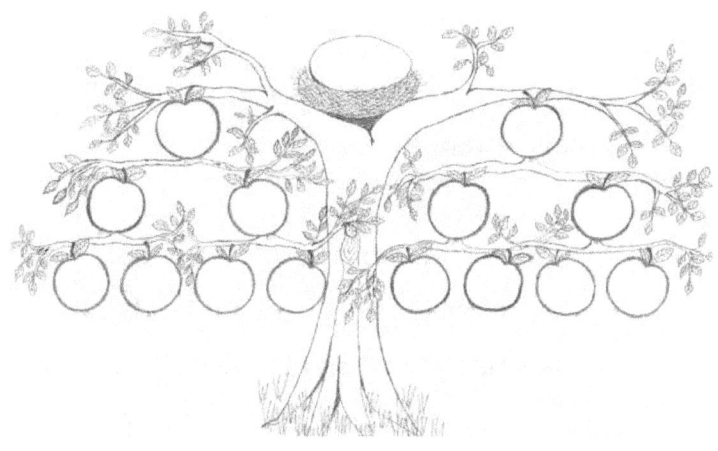

Here is an example of a Family Tree illustration.

Using a template like this you could add names, photographs and birth details, frame it and you have a beautiful piece of family history that everyone would love to own.

(illustration by Lesley M Finch)

TWENTY

Rental House Cleaning and General Maintenance

If you don't mind a bit of heavy duty cleaning, you could offer a service to landlords cleaning rental properties after tenants have moved out.

You could also do a bit of painting, gardening and general maintenance etc. to make the house more attractive to potential tenants.

An empty house will be costing the landlord money in lost rent and an attractive, clean and well maintained house is much easier to find a good tenant for. Speak to the Letting Agents in your area.

TWENTY-ONE

Home Tutoring

Do you have a special skill that you could teach to others? Can you play a musical instrument, are you really good at an academic subject or can you speak a foreign language? If you can do anything like this, you could also teach others your skill.

If you are offering to teach an instrument, advertise in the local music or record store as well as all the other usual places. Never undervalue your talents, charge a fair hourly rate.

TWENTY-TWO

Artists Model

Ask at your local college to see if they are in need of artists models. There are art classes that may need models and it doesn't always need to be 'life' (naked) models. It doesn't matter what shape or size you are, these classes simply need people who can sit quietly in the same position for long periods.

The idea of getting paid for doing nothing sounds like a great idea to me...

TWENTY-THREE

Dog Walking

Another old favorite but you could add a little extra to your service like a daily brushing for all the dogs that you walk. You could provide transport for the dogs that go to day care or offer transport to the dog grooming salon, veterinary office for their regular check-up etc. You could even offer to clean up the yard of dog poop (yuk!).

Be inventive and think of all the things that dog owners hate doing and offer to do it for them.

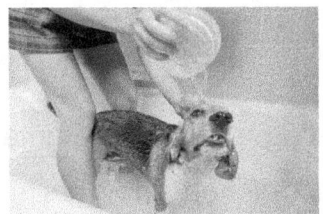

TWENTY-FOUR

Film Extra

Sign up at an agency that offers film extras.

Film extras are the people on TV shows or in films that do not have any speaking parts.

The film and TV show makers need extras of all shapes, sizes and ages to work as extras in their productions.

If you have any special talents make sure that you mention these on your application. Things like horse riding, ice skating, sky diving and so on.

These agencies are not interested in whether you can act or not. They are not are not casting the actors but simply offering extras to the producers.

If you have a talented, unusual or beautiful pet that could take direction in a stressful situation there are agencies that deal specifically in providing animals for films and TV shows.

TWENTY–FIVE

Invent a New TV Show

TV companies are always looking for new and original ideas for a TV show.

When you submit an idea, make sure that you can describe the concept and rules on one sheet of A4 paper.

Just think how much the inventor of 'Millionaire' has made just for thinking up the concept.

Tip: Before you send your idea to a TV company, mail a copy of the letter to yourself making sure you seal it well.

Place the stamp over the area that you have sealed so that, should you need to prove that the idea is yours, it will be obvious when you received the letter in the mail and that the letter has remained unopened.

Do not open the letter when you receive it in the mail, file it away for if you ever need it.

TWENTY-SIX

Make Decorations

If you are a creative person you could make decorations for Christmas, Hallowe'en, Weddings, Bar Mitzvahs, children's parties etc.

You could offer your services to the established event organizers.

Create a sample of the things that you would offer and send photos along with an introductory letter.

TWENTY-SEVEN

Children's Party Organizer

You could offer to organize children's birthday parties. Many parents love the idea of employing a party planner for their children's party.

You could offer to organize themed parties depending on the age of the child.

A teenager's first party without their parents at home is an original idea to use to promote your service.

You can provide the theme, the food, the decoration as well as acting as a chaperone to put the parents mind at rest whilst still allowing the teenager to have a party without parents watching their every move.

TWENTY-EIGHT

Make 'Wedding Stationary Packs'

If you are good at calligraphy or have beautiful handwriting you could do all the invitations, place name cards and seating plans for a wedding. You could also offer to write all the 'thank you' letters for the couple.

You could make the 'wedding favors' and a table centrepiece for each table. Again, you could offer your services to established wedding planners.

TWENTY-NINE

Photography

If you have a good quality camera, you could take some great photographs and put them on the websites that pay you a fee every time someone downloads your photographs.

There are a lot of these websites, so do a Google search to find one that suits you.

Here are a couple to be going on with:

www.istockphoto.com
www.shutterstock.com

You won't be able to buy your new Mercedes with the proceeds.

But, if your photographs are popular, you could have a small monthly income without having to do anything except upload your work to the websites.

I buy some of the photographs that I use in my books from these websites and my sister uses the photographs for her painting. So there is a market for good, interesting photographs.

If you are good with animals, you could advertise your services for taking pet portraits. Pet owners are a great source of business. Most love to have great portraits of their dogs, cats, horses etc.

THIRTY

Home Party Selling

Everyone knows about Home Party Selling through companies like Tupperware.

What about setting up your own Party Plan selling company? Simply source some good quality items that you know people will be interested in, such as candles, crafts, unusual gifts or even pet products.

Never try to sell substandard products or your business won't last past the first couple of parties.

You would only need to buy one example of each product then, when your guests have placed their order, you would buy only what is needed to fill the orders.

Organize a party in your own home inviting all your friends and their friends.

From that first party you should be able to book parties at other people's houses and so on.

Offer a nice incentive to the host of the subsequent parties such as a percentage of the sales for the party or a gift exclusively for the host. Have different value gifts for levels of spend at the party.

This would encourage the host to invite guests that they know will be willing to spend money on the goods that you are selling.

THIRTY-ONE

Design a Board Game

Have you ever looked at the board games that are available in the shops and had a great idea for one of your own? You could design a new and innovative board game using this website.

www.thegamecrafter.com

This is a website that will tell you how to go about getting your board game manufactured. They will also show you how to market your game and will produce the product "on demand". This means that you don't have to have a garage full of your game in the hope that you can sell thousands.

You never know, you may have an idea that will prove to be the next Monopoly!

THIRTY-TWO

Trial New Products

Although this is not strictly a money *making* idea, you will definitely be able to save money by getting products for free in return for giving an opinion on the product.

There are websites where you would sign up and they will send you things in the post to trial.

Things like cosmetics, personal hygiene products and household goods.

It costs nothing to sign up, so you have nothing to lose.

Search online for these websites – there are hundreds, if not thousands needing your opinion.

THIRTY-THREE

Dropshipping

Dropshipping is where you can sell a product that you don't physically have to stock.

You would sign up for one or two of the dropshipping websites and browse their online catalogues. Choose something to sell, maybe on eBay. Set a reasonable price that will give you a nice profit. Once the product is sold, you collect the money from the purchaser, then order the goods and pay for them. The dropshipper would then deliver the goods directly to the purchaser. So you would not have to stock anything, your job is to simply sell the products for a profit.

Once you get the hang of it you can scale it up to create a good sized business.

THIRTY-FOUR

Online Surveys

Online surveys can be a good source of income for housewives, retired people, students etc.

Even people who go out to work can do these surveys in their free time as the survey would usually take around 15-25 minutes to complete and could pay up to $25.

It is very important for any company to do market research to improve its business and to capture more of the market by supplying good products.

Therefore, the market research field is a multi million dollar industry and literally a goldmine.

These companies need impartial, honest and reliable opinions about their services, customers and their clients.

Many companies carry out surveys to find out about the customers demand. In the past this was done by asking people in person about their views and observations for a particular product.

But since the internet entered our lives, the whole process has been automated. Nowadays people don't conduct surveys in person, but instead ask you to share your opinion online about consumer preferences so that the company can make the necessary adjustments to their products or services.

Research companies spend millions of dollars to introduce a new product and all their efforts would be wasted if the product is unable to meet to the needs of the consumers.

To avoid a financial disaster, the research companies will pay people like you to let them know exactly what a consumer would be prepared to buy.

Researchers collect the surveys and try to determine possible public demand by analyzing the data. They use the data collected to understand market demand so that they can create a product, improve it or update it.

Some companies pay the participant in cash whilst others will issue gifts or points that you can exchange for gifts.

There are many survey companies available that will pay you to give your opinion or review about a product they are promoting.

One of the easiest ways to find the online survey companies is to do a search online.

It is wise to do some research before signing up for any of the online survey sites. Some are not as reputable as others.

Visit some of the online forums where people will chat about their experiences with different online survey companies.

Ask questions and make an informed decision about the companies before you sign.

THIRTY-FIVE

Data Entry

If you have good typing or keyboard skills, a computer and an internet connection and some time on your hands you could make some extra cash by doing data entry jobs online.

There are a number of different opportunities, some of which are legitimate whilst others are scams. So be careful which opportunities you sign up for.

There is a genuine opportunity to earn cash but you may find some data entry jobs are not well paid.

It really depends on how fast you can type and what you expect to earn.

For example you could do some forum posting where you are required to post comments on different forums with a link back to your client's website.

You may get paid anything from a couple of cents per post to a couple of dollars.

You can work direct for people you meet on forums such as WarriorForum or DigitalPoint. Or you can join sites such as Odesk or Elance as a freelancer.

The benefit of working from these sites is that they would act as a middleman and some will hold your fee in an Escrow account so you are guaranteed payment on completion of the project.

The downside is that there is a lot of competition from countries like India and the Philippines.

The rates of pay and expectations are a lot lower than those in the UK or the USA.

Never pay a joining fee for a data entry job.

Always remember, if it seems too good to be true, it probably is.

But if you can type or input numbers very quickly, then data entry jobs could be a great way to get some regular income coming into your PayPal account.

THIRTY-SIX

Virtual Assistant

As a virtual assistant you will be expected to complete a range of tasks for your "boss" whom you may never meet or perhaps even speak to in person.

So what does a virtual assistant do?

Well, it depends on your skill set and the job role you take up.

For example some webmasters will employ a virtual assistant to promote their websites.

The VA will sign up to various bookmarking sites and bookmark pages. They may also have to submit RSS feeds to the various aggregators.

Sometimes the virtual assistant will write articles although it is more usual for the virtual assistant to use the articles to promote the site rather than spend time writing them.

They will post them to directories, change them to video or podcasts and generally use them in as many different ways as possible to get links back to the original site.

Some people will employ a virtual assistant to deal with any customer service issues that may arise if they have their own product.

For example they may sell an eBook on Clickbank and would employ someone to monitor the relevant email accounts and answer any queries from potential customers.

There really is no end of tasks that a virtual assistant may complete.

Just be sure that both sides know exactly what is expected.

Lack of communication leads to problems in all relationships and those between virtual assistants and their online bosses are no different.

THIRTY-SEVEN

Affiliate Marketing

If you have access to an internet connection, Affiliate Marketing is a great way for aspiring internet marketers to begin their career.

Affiliate marketing generally means selling the products for another person in return for a commission. It is similar to offline sales where a sales person earns commission for selling products. The only difference here is that all the selling of products or services is done online. You can be an affiliate and promote the product on your website or blog.

Every time you make a sale through the unique affiliate ID link assigned to you at the time of signing up to an affiliate program, you will earn a percentage of commission from that sale.

A good affiliate program will give you a plethora of tools for promoting their products as well as a member's area to keep track of your sales and commissions.

The commission can be in the range of a lowly 10% to a generous 75%. Clickbank.com, Amazon.com and CJ.com are sites that have thousands of products which you can promote as an affiliate.

When you get proficient at this it is quite possible to make a very good income.

Learn all you can before jumping in.

Everything that you want to know about affiliate marketing can be found online.

Don't pay for any report or eBook to find information, take the time to search online and you will find everything that you will ever need to know for free.

WarriorForum.com is a great website to learn all about affiliate marketing. Spend some time just reading all the information on that site and you will soon learn all about the do's and don'ts of internet marketing.

THIRTY-EIGHT

Amazon Mechanical Turk

Amazon Mechanical Turk is a website where webmasters who have certain tasks they want completed will post a job and a price for that job. Then, you can view these jobs and apply for the ones that you are interested in.

So what types of jobs are posted? They vary a lot.

Amazon calls the jobs HITs - Human Intelligence Tasks.

You could be asked to spell check an article for a website or perhaps rewrite an article that was written by someone whose first language isn't' English.

You may be asked to translate from one language into another or comment on the tone of an article.

There is no end to the things that you could do.

How much can you expect to earn?

Well the answer depends on your skills, how fast you can work and the type of HIT you take on.

For example you can expect to be paid more to translate an article than to view one. Some of the HITs are extremely low paid so you need to think in volume. You may be paid one cent per word so how many words could you complete?

The amount of money you could potentially earn is unlimited.

The more you work, the higher the rating you would get which means you are more likely to be considered for the higher paying jobs.

In order to build up your reputation as a good worker, you may have to take on quite a few lowly paid jobs.

You can often make contact with webmasters who after becoming impressed with your work may offer you better paid jobs directly.

If you want to make some money online, Amazon Mechanical Turk is well worth a look.

THIRTY-NINE

Become a Voiceover Artist

There are four main voiceover categories: commercials, narrations, characterizations and imaging. Which one do you think that you would be most suited to?

Buy yourself a microphone. Use a computer to record and playback for practice and critique. You should simply keep on practising your interpretation of the material without focusing on how your voice sounds to you.

There are not many people who enjoy listening to a recording of themselves, so ask for an unbiased opinion from a friend.

Produce a demo and put it on to CD. If you are determined to follow this career path and have a bit of cash available to invest in your future, you may consider having a professional demo done.

Remember that your demo is the first thing an agent will hear and you will only get one chance to make a first impression.

Find talent agencies and companies that may use voiceover artists, like video production houses, smaller ad agencies, radio stations. Call or email them to get the name of the right person to contact. Then send your demo CD with a covering letter and a business card.

If you do not hear anything within a week or two, follow up with a phone call or a letter enquiring if they have received the demo CD.

You could also think about signing with a talent agency or joining an organization of voice over artists but you may be expected to pay a membership fee. Have a look at www.voices.com, they have lots of voice over jobs just waiting for you.

If you are lucky enough to land an assignment, make sure you get a copy of the work, this will serve as a demo CD for the next assignment and should help you to get more work.

FORTY

Translator

Are you able to communicate fluently in more than one language?

Freelance translators can find work very easily these days. With the advent of the internet and the expanding global business market, more and more businesses would be delighted to have the services of a freelance translator.

It is a great asset for any company to be able to hire a translator only when they need it.

You will be able to work from your own home and set work hours that are convenient to you.

Remember, when setting an hourly rate, not to undervalue your talents.

FORTY-ONE

Soap Making

Soap Making is a great hobby but could also become a good earner if you go about marketing your products in the right way.

There are plenty of resources online that will show you how to make good quality soaps, shampoos and body scrubs. It is really easy – I've done it myself!

Before you begin to sell your products you need to check out any legal stuff that needs to be included on your labels. As your products are used on the skin, it is vital to abide by any regulations to avoid any comeback.

Craft fairs are a good place to sell your products.

FORTY-TWO

Sports Event Organizer

This is a money making opportunity that surprised me when I realised the potential cash machine this could be.

If you are good at organizing things then what about organising a cross country race or a cross country cycle race or even a mini marathon etc.

Let's look at the math; 500 entries – $30 paid in advance = $15,000.

Deduct expenses such as permits, advertising, signs, stewards, medals and trophies etc.

You should be left with a nice bit of extra cash either for yourself or for a charity.

Organising a few of these events each year could bring in a good income.

FORTY-THREE

Become a Life Coach

Life coaching is not for everybody.

The most essential characteristic of a potential life coach is an eagerness to help people.

A potential life coach must also be a good listener. If you are the type of person who talks 24/7 then life coaching is not for you.

As a life coach, it is very important to listen to your clients.

You will get all the information that you need through your conversations and if you do not know how to listen, then you will not be able to devise an effective program for the client.

Financially speaking, life coaching could be a good source of income. In fact, a lot of people make a full time living out of being a life coach. You can set your own work hours and only work when the children are in school or in bed.

At the time of writing, there are no formal qualifications needed to set yourself up as a life coach but there are many courses that you can take to enable you to give a good and productive service to your clients.

You could offer your services via telephone or even online or you could set up a small office in your home to facilitate your life coaching business.

So, if you like the idea of helping other people achieve their life's goals, becoming a life coach is a very rewarding job.

FORTY-FOUR

Mystery Shopper

Did you know that you can make money doing something you love like shopping?

Yes there are companies out there that will actually pay you to go and visit their shops and buy something. They usually allow you to keep the purchase too.

Or they could ask you to try out a new restaurant or even an hotel. All they expect in return is that you give them feedback from your visit.

You have to tell them what you liked or didn't like about the experience and how you feel it could have been improved.

Rates of pay will vary from company to company and will depend on what you have to do as part of the job.

You should be told in advance what your remuneration will be.

Some mystery shopping jobs just involve completing a quick survey over the phone or via the internet so the rate of pay for these tasks will be lower.

Others can involve a plane journey or an overnight stay.

Some jobs will require a certain level of expertise in that particular area. For example, you may need a basic understanding of web based shopping in order to test a new e-commerce store.

You should thoroughly research the company as there are plenty of scams online.

But once you find a good, reputable company, there is a real opportunity to combine your love of shopping with earning cash.

The only downside to this money making opportunity is that the work is sporadic. It will not be a regular monthly check.

But, with the right company, you should get enough jobs to supplement your income whilst doing something fun.

FORTY-FIVE

Graphic Designer

If you are skilled at web design you can make a good income online as a graphic designer.

There are a couple of routes open to you.

If you excel at making templates you could design some wordpress or html templates and sell them via the various sites online.

This can build up to a very nice passive income because once you design a popular template you can sell it over and over again.

You could promote your services as a unique graphic designer on sites such as Warrior Forum.com.

You may have to start by offering your service at a very competitive rate in order to build your reputation but you can increase your prices quickly provided you get great feedback from your clients.

You could enter one of the numerous competitions online for those who are interested in graphic design.

Winning one of these contests will help you to establish your name and also build your client book. Just be sure that you are professional at all times.

You could offer unique logo design.

When you set a deadline, exceed your customer's expectations rather than leave them waiting.

As in any service industry, you should always under promise and over deliver.

If you think you can get a new project done in two days, tell your client it will take three and then when you deliver the goods early they will be very impressed.

You can make a lot of money if you have the right skills, attitude and of course some online contacts would help too.

FORTY-SIX

Write Books like This One

Writing books can be a very lucrative occupation.

The usual misconception is that it is impossible to get books published these days. **This is simply not true**.

There is a **guaranteed** way to get your book published **within a couple of weeks**, for around $10. You can have it listed on Amazon about a week after publication.

Then all you have to do is sit back and wait for the monthly royalty checks to arrive.

There is an eBook that you can buy which explains exactly how to make a great income from writing your own books.

The book explains how to get **all of your books** published, the best topics to write about for maximum income and what that income could potentially be.

It also includes sections on where to find the subject information for your books, how to format your book and how to create a book cover.

So, if you have always wanted to be a published author and thought it was impossible – think again.

You could make a full time income simply writing " How to" books and getting them published – and all for a miniscule outlay.

The eBook is only available online at:
http://thenovicewriter.com

FORTY-SEVEN

Personal Assistant

Did you know that you could earn cash from home by becoming an internet based personal assistant?

This type of role is very similar to that of a PA in an office only you work remotely and you may never get to meet your boss in person.

You will chat via Skype and email depending on your respective locations.

The most successful people online are those that have the ability to delegate certain tasks.

They will engage a personal assistant to write articles or to manage their article writers, post the articles to the directories, do social bookmarking and perhaps even answer customer queries by email.

The PA's role is usually to micromanage those boring tasks which are imperative to the success of a business but take up so much time.

The pay can be quite lucrative.

You will need to agree the hours in advance and also a job description.

It is best to have a written agreement as to what the PA is expected to do and by when and also what the boss is expected to do.

All too often busy people will forget that they need ten articles done by tomorrow and will expect their "staff" to drop everything else to get these done.

You can either work full time for one person as a personal assistant or set up an arrangement where you act as a PA to several different people for x number of hours per week.

You should be a well organized person with the usual qualifications required for a secretarial based role.

FORTY-EIGHT

Dressmaking

If you are a talented seamstress/tailor, you could earn some extra cash by taking in alterations.

You could set up a very lucrative business making fancy dress outfits for Halloween, Christmas and all the other occasions where people are looking for an original costume.

No-one wants to arrive at a fancy dress party only to find that there are two other people wearing the same costume. So, someone who can make original 'one off' costumes will be very busy!

You could also make beautiful masks for the masked balls.

FORTY-NINE

Catering

This is another great earner.

If you can put together a delicious buffet, you could offer your services to businesses for their lunchtime meetings.

You could cater for parties, christenings, Bar Mitzvahs, weddings etc. Really the opportunities to expand a catering business are endless.

Create some attractive menus in different price ranges and put them in a nice folder. You will then have something to show prospective clients.

Advertise in your local store, free ad paper and even online on craigslist.

FIFTY

...and finally

There isn't a 50th money making suggestion (49 should be enough to get you started...) but this is where I am going to tell you that simply *reading* this book will not make you the extra cash that you want.

However, if you pick one or two of these ideas and make a start today, you will soon find that you have some extra money to put towards your vacation, tuition, new car or even extra cash to help with the bills.

There are even a few ideas that children could use to earn some extra pocket money.

There are 'thinkers' and 'doers' – which one are you?

I know that you can be successful when you get out there and make a start.

So, what are you waiting for?

Get Started Now!

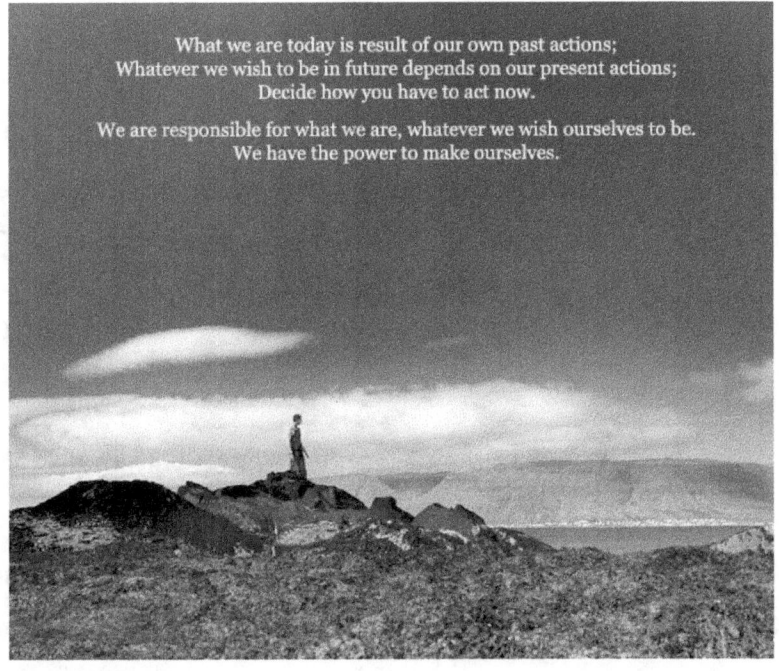

What we are today is result of our own past actions;
Whatever we wish to be in future depends on our present actions;
Decide how you have to act now.

We are responsible for what we are, whatever we wish ourselves to be.
We have the power to make ourselves.

8 Tips to Help you with your New Business

Now that you've decided to start your own business, you might be wondering "How can I get it off to the best possible start?" These tips could help:

1) Set up a working space in your home.

It doesn't matter if this is a small bedroom, one part of the garage, or a corner of the living room. The important thing is to have some space that you can designate as your working area. This will give you the space and room you need to craft your dream.

2) Stock your working space with materials.

This sounds basic perhaps, but one underlying element of success is that you will have easy access to the tools, materials, and other resources you need. Gathering everything close by also keeps you from wasting time searching for it, so this step can be considered a time management strategy, too.

3) Time Management

Define the parameters of your business. What days and hours will you work? When will you market? When will you provide services or products to clients? How will you keep all of this organized?

4) Balance action with planning.

One of the most common pitfalls to successful entrepreneurship is getting too caught up in action without enough planning. The best approach is to plan your next couple of goals and then work backwards to create step by step action plans to reach them. Once you have the plan, then it's time to take the action.

5) Networking.

One of the fastest ways to grow any business is to make connections with other people. Be sure to share your passion and enthusiasm with others at every opportunity. Let people know who you are and what you offer. Remember, people can't buy or use your services if they don't know what you are offering.

6) Present a Professional Image.

If you want to be treated professionally, present a professional image. Set up a separate bank account for your business. Install a separate phone and fax line.

Create professional marketing materials. Be courteous and pleasant in all your customer facing interactions. Basically, be someone people want to do business with.

7) Automate.

Granted, you are just one person (at the moment...) and might have a lot of extra time to take care of all the details. This might work for now, but won't work into the future as you get busier and busier. It's best to set up automatic systems and processes right from the start to free up your time to concentrate on the most profitable activities.

8) Display your Goals.

Write down your goals for your new business, make them colorful and stick them up around your work area. Remember to write them in the present tense.

For example, "it is January 29th and the business has a client base of 50 regular clients".

This will serve to remind you what you are aiming for.

These tips should help to get your home business started (and growing) in the right direction.

May I wish every success in your new venture.

Remember to make a start right now whilst everything is fresh in your mind...